A FAIRY TALE REIMAGINED

The Emperor's New Gender:
A Present-Day Parable of Pluralistic Ignorance

Written by, Vicki Joy Anderson
Edited by, David Arthur

Vicki Anderson
Vicki@ibelongAmen.com

Front Cover Photo by: Pixaby.com

Front Cover Design by: Vicki Joy Anderson

The Emperor's New Gender/Vicki Joy Anderson. – 1st edition

This booklet is dedicated to every acquaintance, co-worker, neighbor, friend, and family member who has ever come into my life, confessing to me a struggle with homosexual temptations or sin.

In a selfish attempt to maintain my status as a "cool Christian"— I put my own desire to be liked ahead of the eternal security of your soul.

After recently re-stumbling upon the Emperor's New Clothes story, I saw myself standing in the comatose crowd of cowardly chanters...and I was deeply convicted of my sin; and of a deficient love that prioritized my own fear of looking like a narrow-minded fool above your heartache and pain.

I have given my life to fervently preaching the gospel to everyone I meet—everyone, I now realize, EXCEPT those who struggle with homosexual temptations. In my attempt to conform to the world's shallow definition of love—I have become both shallow and unloving.

For this, I am deeply repentant. I ask you all for your forgiveness, and I pray for the emancipation of your soul, your healing, your wholeness, and your joy.

VICKI JOY ANDERSON

PREFACE

"The Emperor's New Gender" is a short, 50-page booklet that reimagines Hans Christian Anderson's famous children's tale, "The Emperor's New Clothes," with a postmodern twist! Anderson's tale, originally penned in 1837, still has much to teach us today concerning the woes of what is referred to in social psychology circles as *pluralistic ignorance*—the idea that a person who privately rejects a norm will still go along with it if they believe that everyone else believes it.

In our story, our 21st-century, gender dysphoric Emperor is positioned on a modern stage afront the backdrop of a present-day, PC-movement that is attempting to cow people out of their constitutional rights by rebranding religious freedom, moral convictions, and the preaching of the Gospel as "crimes" and "hate speech."

The story is followed by a two-part *Afterword* explaining the story within its modern context; with an apologetic aimed at both the mainstream American Church, as well as individuals trapped in the LGBTQ movement.

While the book specifically cites a gender-dysphoric emperor, the aim of the book is not to attack individuals in the LGBTQ movement, but rather to highlight the overly-contrived transgender agenda being propagated upon the American people by those with little to no interest whatsoever in LGBTQ rights or the issues and challenges faced by the people involved in its movement.

The book also serves as a cattle prod to the derrière of an increasingly-drowsy Church that has been lulled to sleep by decades of humorous homilies, pep talks, movie clips, and self-esteem gospel messages. The Church that once believed that "Greater love has no one than this, than he who lays down his life for his friends," are now touting to unsaved neighbors and coworkers that, *Love means never having to say you're sorry (for your sin)."*

The Gospel is not politically correct—but it is biblically correct. Christians must learn how to speak the Truth in Love. Many Christians today fall prey to speaking the truth without love; but the second failure is just as dangerous—not speaking up at all. That is why the moral of Anderson's tale still applies today-- namely, the dangers of remaining silent when our conscience convicts us to speak. Once we lose the courage to stand for our convictions, lives and liberties will be lost; and our freedoms will be forfeit.

"If I were to remain silent, I'd be guilty of complicity."

-- Albert Einstein

TABLE OF CONTENTS

The Emperor's New Gender
A FAIRY TALE REIMAGINED

Not so long ago there was an Emperor so exceedingly fond of dressing in drag that he spent all his money on women's clothes so that he could always be dressed like a woman. He cared nothing about his job duties, going to the red-carpet movie premieres, or going for a ride in his Bentley, except to cross dress and show off his new clothes. He had a pair of stilettos for every hour of the day, and instead of saying, as one might, about any other ruler, "The Emperor's taking another phone call," here they always said, "The Emperor's taking another selfie."

In the tolerant city where he lived, life was always gay. Every day many strangers came to town, and among them one day came two swindlers. They let it be known they were a gender dysphoria therapist and a sex reassignment surgeon, and they said they could perform the most magnificent procedures imaginable.

Not only were their hormone therapies and surgical procedures uncommonly state-of-the-art, but men who underwent MTF transitions under their care had a wonderful way of appearing 100% female, except to anyone who was a narrow-minded fool, or who was unusually homophobic.

"These would be just the procedures for me," thought the Emperor. "If I undergo gender reassignment therapy, I would be able to discover which people in my empire are narrow-minded fools. And I could tell the tolerant subjects from the spewers of hate speech. Yes, I certainly must get these procedures done right away." He paid the two swindlers a large sum of money to start work at once.

They set up an office and pretended to practice medicine. The therapist gave the Emperor several bottles of sugar pills and told him to, "take his estrogen pills twice daily." All the money which the therapist and the surgeon demanded went directly form the Emperor's coffers into their PayPal accounts, while the swindlers worked in their office far into the night, photoshopping images of the Emperor.

"I'd like to know how the therapist is getting on with my transition plan," the Emperor mused while looking doubtfully at his manly reflection in a full-length mirror. "He has taken a photo of my progress every week for months. Surely, I must be looking more like a woman by now," the Emperor thought; but he felt slightly uncomfortable when he remembered that those who were narrow-minded fools would not be able to see the changes.

It couldn't have been that he doubted himself, yet he thought he'd rather send someone else to see how things were going.

The whole town knew about these hormone pill's peculiar power, and all were impatient to find out how intolerant their neighbors were.

"I'll send my pastor to the therapist," the Emperor decided. "He'll be the best one to tell me how the progress looks, for he's an honest man and he is under oath to speak the truth in love."

So, the pastor went to the office where the two swindlers sat working away at their laptops. They opened Photoshop and pulled up several dozen *before*-and-*after* shots of the Emperor and showed them to the pastor.

"Heaven help me," thought the pastor as his eyes flew wide open, "I can't see any changes at all." But he did not say so.

Both the swindlers begged him to be so kind as to come near to approve the excellent progress, the beautiful transition. They pointed to the photoshopped images, and the poor old pastor stared as hard as he dared.

4

He couldn't see any changes, because there were no changes to see. "Heaven have mercy," he thought. "Can it be that I'm an intolerant, narrow-minded fool? I'd have never guessed it, and not a soul must know. Am I unfit to be a pastor? It would never do to let on to the Emperor or to my congregation that I can't see the change."

"Don't hesitate to tell us what you think," said the therapist.

"Oh, he's beautiful—he's enchanting!"

"You must respect the pronouns," the swindlers warned.

The old pastor's eyes widened behind his spectacles, fearful he would be found out and his faux pas be branded as hate speech. Imagine what would happen if such word got back to his congregation about their own pastor! What if all the tithers left and went to another church? How would he pay for the new sanctuary expansion and narthex coffee bar without their contributions?

"Such a feminine creature, what curves!" He hastily went on. "I'll be sure to tell the Emperor how delighted I am with *her* progress." He improvised, wiping a bead of sweat from his forehead.

"We're pleased to hear that," the swindlers said. They proceeded to name all the hormones in the Emperor's therapy regime, and to explain the many changes in appearance that would follow his gender reassignment surgery. The old pastor paid the closest attention, so that he could tell it all to the Emperor. And so, he did.

The swindlers at once asked for more money to get on with the therapy. But it all went into their pockets. Not a dime of it went into the Emperor's transition, though they worked at Photoshopping his images as hard as ever.

The Emperor presently sent another trustworthy official to see how the work progressed and how soon he would look like a she. The same thing happened to him that had happened to the pastor.

He looked, and he looked, but as there was no changes to see in the photos, he couldn't see anything but a poorly photoshopped image of the Emperor's head copy/pasted onto a woman's body.

"Isn't it a beautiful success?" the swindlers asked him, as they described the Emperor's soft, round jawline, and her hourglass hips.

"I know I'm not stupid," the man thought, staring in disbelief at the Emperor's protruding Adam's apple, "so it must be that I'm unworthy of my good office. That's strange. I mustn't let anyone find it out, though." So, he praised the feminine features he did not see. He declared he was delighted with the soft facial features and the exquisite figure. To the Emperor he said, "Your photos held me spellbound."

All the town was talking of these splendid photos, and the Emperor wanted to see them for himself. Attended by a band of chosen men, among whom were his two trusted officials—the ones who had previously been to the therapist's office—he set out to see the two swindlers. He found them copying and pasting with might and main, but none of their images reflected that of his own mirror.

"Magnificent," said the two officials already duped. "Just look, Your Majesty, what precision! What feminine beauty!"

They pointed to the laptop screens, each supposing that the others could see the changes.

"What's this?" thought the Emperor. "I can't see anything. I still look like a man. This is terrible! Am I a narrow-minded fool? Am I unfit to be a champion of the LGBTQ movement? What a thing to happen to me of all people!"

But when pressed, he declared, "Oh! I am so *very* pretty!" And he nodded enthusiastically at the photoshopped images. Nothing could make him say that he couldn't see the changes.

His whole retinue stared and stared. One saw no more than another, but they all joined the Emperor in exclaiming, "Oh! She is so *very* pretty," and they advised him that once his transition was complete, that he should wear his finest dress and heels and parade down the streets as the guest of honor in the city's annual LGBTQ Pride Parade.

"Magnificent! Excellent! Unsurpassed!" were bandied from mouth to mouth, and everyone did his best to seem well pleased. The Emperor gave each of the swindlers a rainbow flag pin to wear in his buttonhole, and the title of "Sir Sycophant."

Several years later, it was time for the final step in the process—gender reassignment surgery. The swindlers set up a top-secret operating room which no one, including the Emperor, could enter. The surgeon put the Emperor under anesthesia and wheeled him into the empty OR.

The townsfolk stood outside in front of massive jumbotrons watching CNN with bated breath. Journalists stood outside the operating room door, listening to the clank and grind of the surgeon's tools and drills.

Many hours later, the surgeon emerged from the OR covered in sweat. And at last he said, "Now the Emperor is at last an Empress!"

Then the cameras panned to the Emperor *herself* and the surgeon raised an arm and pointed to the Emperor and said, "Look at her breasts, her hips, and her beautiful long hair," pointing out each new feminine feature.

"She is the most beautiful woman in the kingdom. One would almost think she had been born this way, but that is what makes her so extraordinary."

This was met with deafening cheers and accolades from the bystanders watching the monitors outside; and despite not seeing one physical change to the Emperor's appearance, no one accused the surgeon or the news crew of reporting fake news, for all feared being branded a narrow-minded fool.

"Bravo!" cheered all the noblemen standing amongst the crowd, though they could see no change either, for there were no changes to see.

Some time passed, and the day of the annual LGBTQ Pride Parade finally arrived. Just before the procession, the swindlers said, "If Your Imperial Majesty will condescend to remove her dress, we will help you on with your parade costume here in front of the long mirror."

The Emperor undressed, and the swindlers waxed his chest and put on his makeup. Then came his wig, his high heels, his padded bra, and his Spanx—one garment after another. They colored in his brows and taped back his ears. They cinched his waist and put him in a gown.

Then they took him around the waist and fastened something—that was his train—as the Emperor spun round

11

and round before the looking glass, squealing and clapping his hands in glee.

"How womanly Your Majesty looks. Isn't she beautiful!" He heard on all sides, "That figure, so perfect! Those facial features, so feminine! It is a magnificent transformation."

Then the minister of public processions entered the room and announced: "Your Majesty, your float is waiting outside."

"Well, I'm supposed to be ready," the Emperor said, and turned again for one last look in the mirror. "It is a remarkable transition, isn't it?" He seemed to regard his appearance with the greatest interest.

The noblemen who were to carry his train stooped low and reached for the floor and picked up his mantle.

The Emperor curtsied, and they bowed, pretending she was a queen. They didn't dare admit that he still looked like a king.

So off went the Emperor in procession under his splendid canopy. Everyone in the streets and the windows said, "Oh, how fine is the Emperor's new gender! Don't her new features fit her to perfection? No one would ever know she was born a man!"

Nobody would confess that they could still see broad shoulders bulging beneath her tight sequin gown, or the Adam's apple protruding from her large neck. The crowd clapped their hands, while wincing at the largesse of the Empress' hands waving back at them. The jumbotrons magnified her prominent brow ridge, large torso, and her sizeable thigh gap. But no one said a word for fear that it would prove them to be a narrow-minded fool.

No, in fact, no transgender attempt had ever been such a complete success!

"That chick is a dude!" a little child said. "The Empress is a man in drag!"

"Did you ever hear such a conspiracy theory?" said its father. And one person whispered to another what the child had said, "*The Empress is a man.* A child says she is just a man in a dress."

"The Empress is a man! He is a man in drag!" the whole town cried out at last.

The Emperor began to shake, his size-12 feet quaking in the tight confines of his 5" heels, for he suspected they were right. But he thought, "This procession has got to go on. In the name of progress, sexual freedom, and tolerance—this procession MUST go on!" So, he walked with more pride than ever, as his noblemen held high his rainbow-flag train, believing the entire city to be nothing but a bunch of narrow-minded fools.

The End

AFTERWORD
A FAIRY TALE DECIPHERED

I am amazed that you are so quickly deserting Him who called you by the grace of Christ, for a different gospel; which is really not another; only there are some who are disturbing you and want to distort the gospel of Christ. But even if we, or an angel from heaven, should preach to you a gospel contrary to what we have preached to you, he is to be accursed! As we have said before, so I say again now, if any man is preaching to you a gospel contrary to what you received, he is to be accursed! For am I now seeking the favor of men, or of God? Or am I striving to please men? If I were still trying to please men, I would not be a bond-servant of Christ.

Galatians 1:6-10 (NASB)

A Word to Those Chanting with the Crowd

The Emperor's New Gender is a modern retelling of Hans Christian Anderson's renowned tale, *The Emperor's New Clothes*. Anderson did not pen his tale as an attempt to attack naked emperors; but rather, his fable was an expose on what happens to a culture once its individuals abandon their personal freedoms and convictions and fall victim to social engineering. The Emperor's kingdom is a society that adopts credos like, "Majority rules." It is a nation that changes its military slogan from, "Be all you can be" to "Army of One." It is groupthink. It is the Hive, the Collective, the Borg.

In Matthew 24:7, Jesus tells us that the generation alive to witness his second coming will be living "as it was in the days of Noah." In Noah's day, tens of thousands, if not hundreds of thousands, of people were forewarned of a pending cataclysm.

Amongst the masses, only eight people took heed and made life-saving preparations for themselves. Talk about being in the minority!

But whose side would you have rather been on when that first flash of lightening peeled across the sky? Noah's, of course! But Noah's safety through the storm came at great personal sacrifice. The Scriptures tell us that he spent one hundred years constructing the ark, during which time he endured unceasing jeers and mockery from everyone around him. He was the proverbial *narrow-minded fool* of our story.

The story of Noah's ark is an apropos example of the fallacy behind *Argumentum ad populum*—the argumentation theory that postulates that an idea or point-of-view must be correct because the majority of people believe it to be true.

But majority opinion does not override reality!

If every single human being alive on planet Earth agreed that the sky is made of lead—the sky would not suddenly turn to lead; just as the Emperor in our story does not magically become a different gender just because a couple of swindlers tell him so, and a crowd of enablers cheer him on.

The Emperor's New Gender is a modernized version of Anderson's tale; a version that those of us living in the 21st century can better resonate with—but just as Anderson did not pen his tale as an attempt to attack naked emperors; neither is this story an attempt to attack people in the LGBTQ movement.

Rather, it is a fair warning to believers (the "folks in the crowd") to work out their salvation with fear and trembling; because whichever character you find yourself relating to in this story is more than likely where you will be standing should you ever wake up to find yourself living "in the days of Noah."

Do you want to be one of the chanting chumps caught up in the crowd; or do you want to be the lone childlike voice of Truth that rises above the din of docility?

Galatians 1:6-10 tells us there is ONE gospel. The gospel we share with people who lie, cheat, and steal is the same gospel we share with Atheists, Wiccans, murderers, porn addicts, alcoholics, fornicators, and adulterers. Regardless of the varying sins and addictions that plague the people of Earth, we offer them all the same gospel formula:

All have sinned and fall short of the glory of God (Romans 3:23); and Jesus Christ is the Way, the Truth, and the Life, no one comes to the Father except through Him (John 14:6). To preach any other gospel, according to Galatians 1:6, is tantamount to *deserting Christ!*

But is this the gospel that the mainstream Church in America is encouraging us to preach to the people in the LGBTQ movement? Are the churches preaching sin and repentance? No, because the *Beelzeborg* has rebranded the Good News as *hate speech* and the Church is being forced to drink their pablum.

The Word of God is being overwritten before our very eyes by a steady stream of *newspeak*, thus lulling believers into accepting that people who struggle with homosexual temptations, by nature of being "born that way," are exempt from the Gospel.

But is it true?

Is the "born that way" argument sound hermeneutics, or is it merely a textbook example of transitive logic? Transitive logic states that if A equals B, and B equals C, then A must equal C.

In other words: if a person is created in the image of God, then any innate desires and proclivities they are born with are a part of their personhood.

And because God knit us together in our mother's wombs and created us in His image; any proclivities or desires that we are born with will fall under the umbrella of God's approval. After all, it wouldn't be just for God to hardwire desires into our nature, and then condemn us to hell for carrying out those desires—would it?

This is the bottom line question: Is it just for God to condemn people for carrying out the cravings of their flesh if they were born with those fleshly cravings?

Ephesians 2:3 says, "Among them we too all formerly lived in the lusts of our flesh, indulging the desires of the flesh and of the mind, and were by nature children of wrath, even as the rest."

So, if all of us, by nature, are born with sinful desires and cravings, whether those desires and cravings are for adultery, murder, sexual promiscuity, or homosexual acts, it makes little difference. It simply does not make sense to say that some fleshly cravings are deserving of God's wrath, while others are not.

If our bottom line question is the justice of God, we really are at a Catch 22. Because how is it just to hold all of mankind accountable for the cravings of their flesh, but to give people with the urge to participate in homosexual acts (and no one else) a free pass?

We either have to believe that every single one of us (regardless of temptations and sin) are expected to make

war with our flesh and overcome evil with good; or that it is required of none of us at all and the message of Galatians 1 and Ephesians 2, and the entirety of Scripture, are the mere rantings of hyper-religious homophobes.

Friends, the gospel we preach to people who do not struggle with homosexual temptations, is, in fact, the exact same gospel that we should be preaching to the people who do; because, according to the inspired Word of God, we are all children of wrath—by nature.

Or, to put it in modern terms: We are all *born that way*. (Or, "born into sin" or "born with a sin nature"). Some theologians say, "We are shaped by iniquity," which literally reads: We are born into perversion. We are ALL born into perversion!

Yes, "God is love," but this does not mean that God will not hold every single one of us accountable for the choices that we make.

We have all been given the gift of choice; but the Word of God attaches an irrevocable eternal responsibility to every choice we make, so we must choose wisely.

This is where the rubber meets the road. This is the litmus test for determining who you are in the Emperor's kingdom. What gospel are you preaching to the LGBTQ people in your life? Is it the same gospel you are preaching to your alcoholic friends? Your promiscuous friends? Your friend who cheats on his taxes?

Or is the gospel you are preaching to your LGBTQ friends and acquaintances a watered-down, kid-glove, PC-version of the gospel that lacks actual saving power by sparing them from being labeled a *sinner?*

Because Paul tells us in Galatians 1:6-10 that *that* gospel is really no gospel at all and, furthermore, that those who preach such a gospel fall under a curse!

If we preach a different gospel to those in the LGBTQ movement, we are not preaching the gospel to them at all. In fact, we are *withholding* the gospel from them!

Think of it another way. What if Jesus Christ came to earth and instead of preaching the gospel, he revealed every cause of cancer. He named Christians as the gatekeepers of this knowledge and the Church was commanded to go and tell as many people as possible.

If the Church took that knowledge to every nation, every hospital, every doctor, every nurse, every scientist, every cancer patient, every family member, neighbor, coworker, and friend—everyone _except_ people in the LGBTQ movement—would that behavior be categorized as tolerant or homophobic?

Paul concluded Galatians 1:6-10 by admitting that he could not simultaneously be both a people pleaser and a servant of Christ. His choice to be a servant of Christ, by default, made him unpopular with the general public.

In the same sense that Paul warned that we cannot be both people pleasers and servants of God; neither can we be both politically correct and biblically correct.

We must choose.

There is only one difference in the Emperor's story between every man and woman in the crowd and the one outspoken child. It wasn't that the child knew the Emperor was a man, and no one else did. They all knew he was a man—every last one of them! The difference is that the child spoke up. His voice was heard while all others were stifled—stifled by fear of looking like a narrow-minded fool.

William Shakespeare once wrote, "A coward dies a thousand times before his death, but the valiant taste of death but once" (Julius Caesar).

The deaths that Shakespeare is talking about here is not physical death, but the inner deaths of our soul every time we betray our own conscience.

The writer of Hebrews warns us that in these crossroad moments—the proverbial "angel on one shoulder, devil on the other"—to heed the voice of God's spirit and to not harden your heart (Hebrews 3:7-8).

So what does any of this have to do with the Church and its relationship with the people trapped in the LGBTQ movement?

A decade ago, the Borg told the Church that a "baby" in the womb is not a baby, it is a blob of tissue. Now we are being told *boy* can mean *girl*, and *girl* can mean *boy*.

The next totem up the pole is to introduce post-genderism to the masses, which is the idea that gender is an arbitrary, needlessly limiting label and should be abandoned altogether.

Next will be the integration of A.I., which will eventually lead to Transhumanism (or post-humanism, H+, or Singularity)—the DNA-altered rebirth of the human race that reflects the image of the Beast instead of the image of God.

This battle is not against flesh and blood! In other words, the battle is not between homosexual sin and fornication between a man and a woman, nor is it between the LGBTQ movement and the Church. The Collective in charge of the Singularity agenda are swindlers.

They do not care about those who identify as homosexual, transgender, they-gender, a-gender, or gender-fluid; and they especially do not care about their rights or freedoms.

People trapped in the LGBTQ movement are mere pawns in their larger agenda. Once the Collective moves on to post-genderism, and ultimately Singularity, the people in the LGBTQ movement will be stripped of their courage awards and abandoned.

The cheering crowd-for-hire will move on to applaud the next socially-engineered phase of the mission. And make no mistake, the Collective is not on a mission to empower the LGBTQ movement; they are on a mission to wipe the image of God off the face of the earth.

If we merely stand amidst the LGBTQ crowd chanting with the masses, it will only become more difficult to stand up against the next onslaught against Biblical truth—

and it is coming.

Our very lives depend upon our courage. We must continue to believe that the Gospel is the GOOD NEWS and we must preach it indiscriminately to EVERYONE.

I solemnly charge you in the presence of God and of Christ Jesus, who is to judge the living and the dead, and by His appearing and His kingdom: preach the word; be ready in season and out of season; reprove, rebuke, exhort, with great patience and instruction. For the time will come when they will not endure sound doctrine; but wanting to have their ears tickled, they will accumulate for themselves teachers in accordance to their own desires and will turn away their ears from the truth and will turn aside to myths.

2 Timothy 4:1-4 (NASB)

A Word to Those Who Have Walked a Mile in the Emperor's Shoes

The Emperor is not the "bad guy" of this story. The Emperor merely made a series of life choices, which two swindlers capitalized upon for their own gain; and he only increased in his commitment to those choices after being supported and applauded by an inner circle of friends and confidantes, and ultimately, his entire community.

Modern society has divvied up humanity into an endless myriad of polarizing categories; but the Bible is unabashedly non-binary when it comes to pigeonholing the entire human race. Every single human being falls into one, solitary category: *Sinner.*

Let's level the playing field—every one of us has at one point in our life walked in the Emperor's shoes. No matter how you choose to personally identify yourself, the Bible categorizes all of us collectively as "enemies of God" (Romans 5:10), and the Bible only provides one formula for being transferred from the enemy column to the friend column. We all, regardless of our particular proclivities, must repent of our sin, surrender our lusts, and trust in Christ alone to impute (credit) his righteousness to us on Judgment Day.

Romans 3:10-12 says:

THERE IS **NONE** RIGHTEOUS, **NOT EVEN ONE**;

THERE IS **NONE** WHO UNDERSTANDS,

THERE IS **NONE** WHO SEEKS FOR GOD;

ALL HAVE TURNED ASIDE, **TOGETHER** THEY HAVE BECOME

USELESS;

THERE IS **NONE** WHO DOES GOOD,

THERE IS **NOT EVEN ONE**."

Summary: God lumps ALL of humanity—past, present, and future—into ONE category.

Furthermore, what does Paul mean when he says, "all have turned aside?" You might be surprised to learn that the

1828 Webster's dictionary defines the word *pervert* (verb) as: *to turn*. This flies in the face of the contemporary usage of the word, where *pervert* (now a noun) is a judgmental slur reserved for sexual deviants such as pedophiles, rapists. sodomites, sadomasochists, homosexuals, and Peeping Toms. Lest you think the word has merely etymologized over the past century, the 2018 definition offered on Dictionary.com is: *to turn away from the right course; to lead into mental error or false judgment.*

Viewed through the lens of Romans 3:10-12, coupled with the actual definition of the word: every human being can be classified as a pervert; because every one of us, before receiving salvation, "turned aside" from "the right course" of God's covenant and laws "into mental error and false judgment."

God's standard of sexual purity was not raised solely above people who practice homosexual acts, it was unfurled over every single human being to ever live. According to the non-categorical description of humanity laid out in Romans 3:10-12, the Emperor doesn't have to be naked, transgender, gender dysphoric, non-binary, queer, or homosexual—all he has to be is human.

The devastating feature of the Emperor's story is not that he wore a dress and heels; it is that he was swindled. How interesting that Anderson introduces two swindlers into the story as the Emperor's primary antagonists. This is reminiscent of the Garden of Eden, where Adam and Eve (with their still- dormant, yet existing, free wills intact) were also swindled—by a serpent. A serpent who knew the innate desires and cravings of Adam and Eve's flesh better than they yet knew them themselves, and he exploited this for his own personal gain.

While we are all accountable for our free will choices, it doesn't negate the fact that we must wrestle against an unseen spiritual realm full of sadistic, soul-swindlers who are working tirelessly at every moment to draw us into darkness—lulling us down their broad breadcrumb byway that leads to destruction (Matthew 7:13).

Even though Romans 3:10-12 tells us a total of eight times that ALL of us are unified in our apathy towards righteousness, the serpent (our Adversary) attempts to polarize us into factions and categories so that we feel misunderstood, discriminated against, and isolated.

For this reason, many people who struggle with homosexual temptations have been swindled into believing the serpent's lie that they are the only ones being required by God to give up their sexual preferences and liberties upon receiving Christ as their Savior.

Nothing could be farther from the truth!

Even those who have never had homosexual temptations or sin in their life must also lay down their affairs, their promiscuity, their non-believing girlfriend or boyfriend, their divorce proceedings, their open marriage, as well as any lustful habits such as masturbation, pornography, sexual fantasies, immodest dress, inappropriate flirtation or harassment, and the like.

Man or woman, one thing is clear, NO ONE is left unaltered after receiving Jesus Christ as Lord and Savior.

Romans 6 explains that when we come to Christ, our old self dies with Christ in his death and that we are no longer slaves to sin. We are then raised with Christ in his resurrection ("born again") where we are set free. Not free to sin or do whatever we want, but free from the old self which was a slave to the flesh.

When our old self dies, it must shed old habits, sins, patterns, strongholds, and addictions. Going from death to life is the ultimate seismic shift. If that seismic shift is not apparent after conversion,

I would seriously question the validity of that conversion; because being a slave to our flesh does not in any way resemble being a slave to Christ's righteousness.

Putting on the robe of Christ's righteousness is what frees us from the nakedness of sin. The Romans believed they had found a loophole after Christ's death (Romans 6:1). They believed that because their sins were now so freely

forgiven that the more they sinned, the more Christ would be glorified (because every time they sinned, they afforded Christ an opportunity to display his mercy).

But the freedom that Christ died to give us was freedom from the curse of sin and death (Romans 8:1-2), not freedom to continue in our sin.

But the good news is, there IS a loophole!

The "loophole" is not that God won't hold us accountable for our sin because he loves us so much; or that our sin won't be considered sin if we are born that way.

The loophole is the cross.

The cross frees us from the curse of the law—the deserved death sentence brought on by our sin, and the consequences of an eternity in hell.

No one goes to hell *because* they engage in homosexual acts. If someone who engaged in homosexual sin here on earth one day finds themselves in hell, they will be there for the exact same reason that everyone else is there—they

refused to turn from their sin or to trust in Christ alone for their salvation.

But hell can be avoided because Christ's death provided a loophole in the covenant. His shed blood allowed a just God to alter the original law of sin and death to allow repentant sinners to live forever.

This is the Gospel.

The Gospel is not *hate speech*—

it is a love letter from your Creator!

It is the Good News.

It is the eternal cure for soul cancer.

It is the pardon issued the hour before the gallows.

And it is *yours* for the asking.

"Always be ready to give an answer..."

1 Peter 3:15

If you feel isolated, alone, confused, and misunderstood, reach out to us today. Share with us your prayer requests, your questions; or share with us a praise report or a testimony. We are just an e-mail away.

Contact Vicki Joy
Vicki@ibelongAmen.com

Or David
DavidArthur@ibelongAmen.com

I Belong, Amen! Ministries
PO Box 854
Mount Vernon, OH 43050
www.ibelongAmen.com

Made in the USA
Lexington, KY
13 January 2019